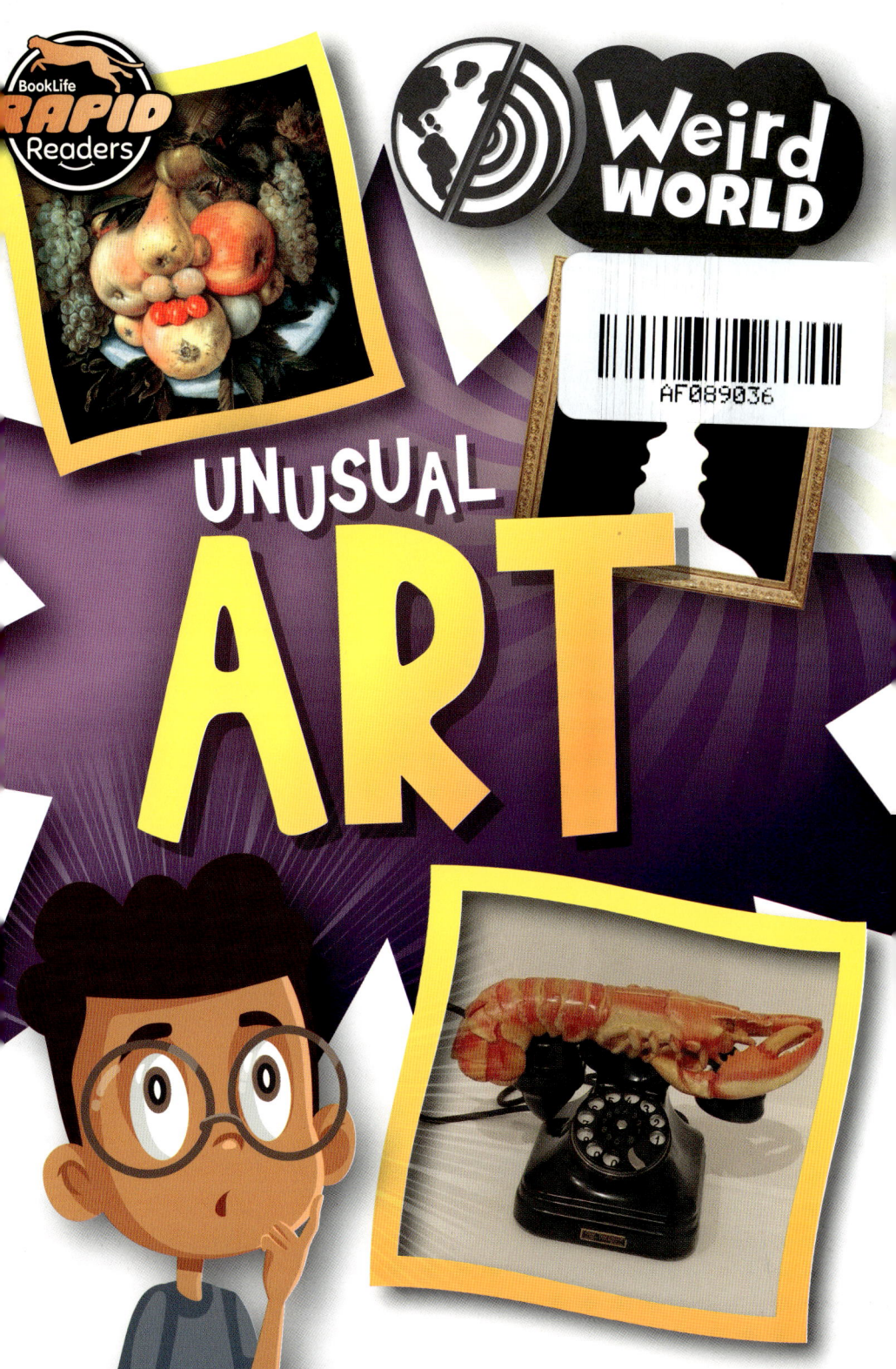

BookLife
PUBLISHING

©2023
BookLife Publishing Ltd.
King's Lynn, Norfolk
PE30 4LS, UK

All rights reserved.
Printed in China.

A catalogue record for this book is available from the British Library.

ISBN: 978-1-80505-017-9

Written by:
Hermione Redshaw
Adapted by:
Rebecca Phillips-Bartlett
Edited by:
Elise Carraway
Designed by:
Isabella Croker

FSC MIX
Paper from responsible sources
FSC® C113515
www.fsc.org

All facts, statistics, web addresses and URLs in this book were verified as valid and accurate at time of writing. No responsibility for any changes to external websites or references can be accepted by either the author or publisher.

AN INTRODUCTION TO BOOKLIFE RAPID READERS...

Packed full of gripping topics and twisted tales, BookLife Rapid Readers are perfect for older children looking to propel their reading up to top speed. With three levels based on our planet's fastest animals, children will be able to find the perfect point from which to accelerate their reading journey. From the spooky to the silly, these roaring reads will turn every child at every reading level into a prolific page-turner!

CHEETAH
The fastest animals on land, cheetahs will be taking their first strides as they race to top speed.

MARLIN
The fastest animals under water, marlins will be blasting through their journey.

FALCON
The fastest animals in the air, falcons will be flying at top speed as they tear through the skies.

Photo Credits

Images are courtesy of Shutterstock.com. With thanks to Getty Images, Thinkstock Photo and iStockphoto.
RECURRING – Amovitania, bansenn, RidiUmbrella. COVER – Volodymyr Krasyuk, Martin Janecek, Nicoleta Ionescu, bansenn, Venera_I, RidiUmbrella, Carpediem6655, Nacaru. 4–5 – Patrick Wang, Pixel-Shot, Milano M, Mehaniq, VIS Fine Art, Puripat Lertpunyaroj. 6–7 – Kseniya Shturmina, Sahaib, Nacaru. 8–9 – mosman.photo, EdgarMueller. 10–11 – SL-Photography, Martin Janecek, SKart74. 12–13 – StockSmartStart, JarektUploadBot, Carpediem6655. 14–15 – MasterPhoto, Coltty, Noel V. Baebler, Isa Fernandez Fernandez, Pixel-Shot. 16–17 – imaginasty, PhotoExpozure, Patche99z. 18–19 – Baloncici, Alexey_Erofejchev. 20–21 – Africa Studio, Triin Kepler, Ann Keyvan. 22–23 – Pressmaster, Lopolo.

CONTENTS

Page 4	Weird and Wonderful
Page 6	Lobster Telephone
Page 8	Fancy Floors
Page 10	Is That What I Think It Is?
Page 12	Making Faces Out of Food
Page 14	Eco Art
Page 16	Mud Maid
Page 18	Traffic Light Tree
Page 20	Art Out Loud
Page 22	Unusual Art
Page 24	Glossary and Index

Words that look like *this* are explained in the glossary on page 24.

WEIRD and WONDERFUL

Art is all around us.

Art can be beautiful.
Art can be interesting.

But some art? Some art is unusual.

Are you ready to see some weird and wonderful art?

You will question everything you know about the world of art.

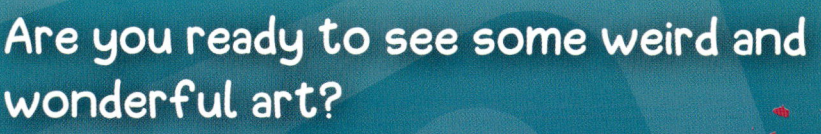

LOBSTER TELEPHONE

In 1938, Salvador Dalí created the Lobster Telephone.

Salvador Dalí

The Lobster Telephone is a piece of Surrealist art.

Surrealist artists often put random items together in a strange way.

Surrealist art is meant to free people's minds.

FANCY FLOORS

Why should amazing art stay stuck inside?

Many street artists go outside and use chalk to draw on pavements.

Some artists make 3D street art. This art can make it look like the ground has changed underneath you.

IS THAT What I THINK It Is?

Some artists use illusions to trick your eyes into seeing something different from what is really there.

Look at this illusion by Edgar Rubin. What do you see?

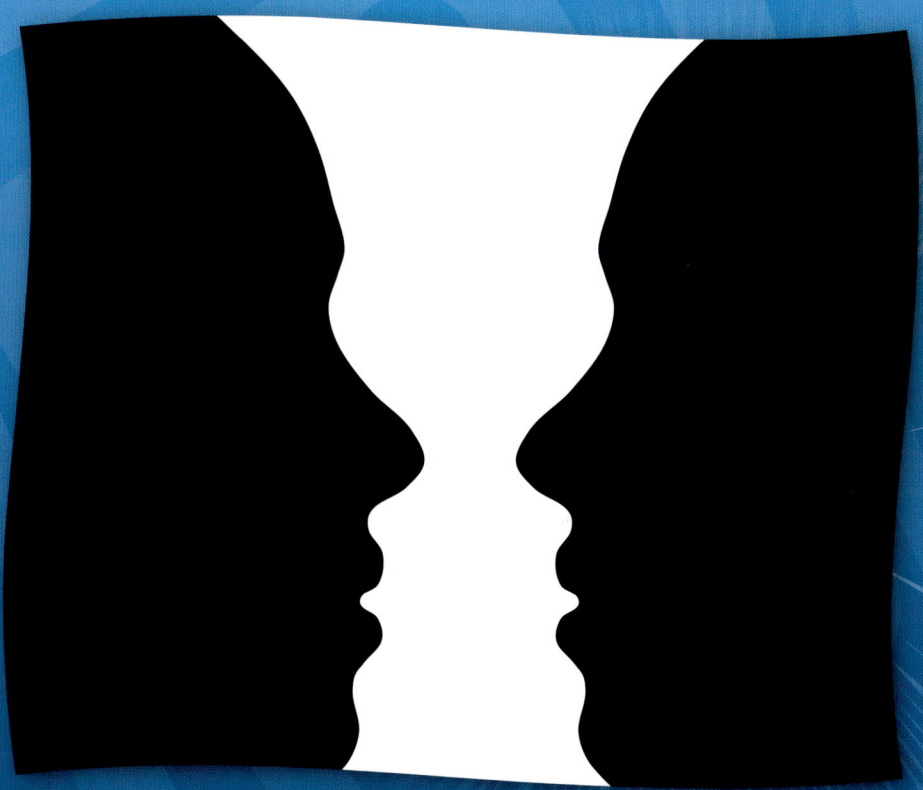

Some people see two faces. Other people see a cup.

MAKING FACES OUT of FOOD

Giuseppe Archimboldo was a painter. He painted <u>portraits</u>.

These portraits were very unusual. The faces were made out of food!

Thinking it cannot get any weirder?
Turn this book upside down!

Now they just look like bowls of fruit and vegetables.

ECO ART

Some pieces of art spread important messages.

This <u>sculpture</u> of an <u>endangered</u> animal was made by Artur Bordalo using rubbish.

Many artists make art using rubbish to make people think about the environment.

Have you ever made art out of waste?

MUD MAID

The Mud Maid is a living sculpture. She was made by a brother and sister called Sue and Pete Hill.

The Mud Maid is covered in real plants.

Different plants grow at different times of year, so she is always changing.

TRAFFIC LIGHT TREE

In London, there is a strange set of traffic lights. These lights are not as helpful as normal traffic lights.

This sculpture by Pierre Vivant has 75 sets of lights. They change in a random order. Many drivers find it confusing!

Art Out Loud

Music is a type of art.

John Cage is known for an unusual piece of music called Living Room Music.

Cage used everyday items as musical instruments.

He showed that you could make music using items from around your house.

UNUSUAL ART

From lobsters on phones to fruit basket faces to people made out of mud, some art is very unusual.

What unusual art would you like to see? Gather your weirdest art supplies and get creative!

GLOSSARY

3D	three-dimensional, has width, height and depth
endangered	in danger of going extinct
environment	the natural world
portraits	paintings, drawings or photographs of a person
sculpture	a piece of art that is made by carving or moulding a material

INDEX

animals 14
artists 7–10, 15
chalk 8
London 18

plants 17
rubbish 14–15
vegetables 13